CW00449437

The Ethi(

Transplantation

Keith M Rigg

Consultant Transplant Surgeon,
Nottingham City Hospital NHS Trust and
Reader, St Helens, Burton Joyce

GROVE BOOKS LIMITED
RIDLEY HALL RD CAMBRIDGE CB3 9HU

Contents

Acknowledgments

I would like to thank Rick Simpson and Harriet Harris of the Grove Ethics Group for their helpful comments and suggestions on successive drafts. I would also like to give special thanks to my family for their encouragement, support and 'computer time' as I have undertaken this work.

The Cover Illustration is by Peter Ashton

First Impression October 2001
ISSN 1470-854X
ISBN 1 85174 479 7

1
Introduction: Outlining the Issues

Organ transplantation has become standard medical practice over the last 40 years and with it has arisen an increasing number of ethical issues. These have occurred as increasing numbers of patients require organ transplantation and new technologies have developed, whilst at the same time fewer donor organs are available. Provision is also vastly different within the global community and universal provision of transplantation is not available.

Medical, legal and ethical boundaries are being pushed back in an attempt to satisfy the various demands. Throughout this booklet I will endeavour to present a balanced view of the issues, whilst acknowledging that I address them as a Christian and a transplant surgeon. As with other ethical areas there are often no clear-cut answers and it is therefore important to work from and apply basic principles. In this introductory chapter I will give a factual overview of transplantation, consider the key ethical issues and develop an ethical framework. Subsequent chapters will look at these ethical issues from the donor (chapter 2) and recipient perspective (chapter 3) and briefly at further issues which developments in medicine are creating (chapter 4) before drawing some conclusions (chapter 5).

Overview of Transplantation

Solid organs (kidney, heart, lung, liver, pancreas and small bowel) and tissues (cornea, heart valves, bone marrow, bone, skin, the insulin-producing islet cells of the pancreas and composite grafts eg the hand) can and have all been transplanted. The history of successful solid organ transplantation is relatively recent with the first kidney transplant being performed in 1954, heart in 1967, liver in 1963, lung in 1963, pancreas in 1966 and small bowel in 1967. Over this period of time, the success rates for all transplants has steadily improved owing to better techniques, new technologies, a greater understanding of how the body interacts with foreign organs and tissues, and the development of drugs to combat rejection.

At the same time people are living longer and expectations are higher. Transplantation, as a treatment option, is therefore available to an increasing number of people with end-stage organ failure. Organ failure of the heart and liver, for example, will lead to death unless a transplant is performed. Kidney failure is best treated with a transplant although the patient can be supported by dialysis with a resultant inferior quality of life. Although the number of patients with these conditions is small and not everyone is suitable for a transplant, it is inevitable that some will be successfully transplanted whilst others will die. As a result of these stark choices the demand for transplantation is increasingly greater than the supply. Only 30–40% of patients with kidney failure will be suitable for transplantation. In the UK each year only 1,700 patients have a kidney transplant, whilst over 5,500 are waiting for one because of insufficient organs.

Cadaveric and live donors are the two sources of organs for transplantation. Cadaveric organs come from patients who have died, usually in an intensive care unit, and where the family have given permission for the organ to be used. Live donor organs usually come from family members who have offered one organ, or part of an organ, to their loved one.

Developing an Ethical Framework

Technological advances in healthcare, coupled with greater patient expectation, have often meant that new treatments are developed and implemented without due regard to ethical and resource implications. The prevailing question of the day is 'Can it be done?' rather than 'Should it be done?' Just because there is the technology and ability to undertake some form of treatment does not always mean that it should be done. This is one of the key ethical questions facing healthcare today and it is very relevant for transplantation. It is therefore important to explore all the ethical areas touched on by transplantation and to develop an ethical framework that can be applied to the specific questions raised in practice.

What Ethical Principles Can Be Used to Develop a Framework?

There are few specific references to contemporary medical ethical issues in Scripture and in particular there are no references to transplantation. The Old Testament has enshrined within it the moral responsibility of humankind and the succinct expression of this is the Ten Commandments. Although the latter six commandments are summed up as 'Love your neighbour as yourself' (Leviticus 19.18) it is worth noting the specifics of four of these commandments—you shall not murder, you shall not steal, you shall not bear false witness and you shall not covet. These are all relevant in considering the various aspects of the ethics of transplantation. In the New Testament Jesus again summarizes the Ten Commandments with the basic tenets of loving God and loving our neighbour as ourselves. Throughout the New Testament there is an emphasis on loving God and humankind, manifested as obedience to God, self-giving and service. The whole of humankind is equal in God's sight and the principles of justice and respect for all regardless of social standing, gender or race are also found throughout the Scriptures.

There are four accepted principles of secular medical ethics: autonomy, non-maleficence, beneficence and justice. These secular principles can be linked with the above biblical principles, although conflicts can arise. For example, the principle of autonomy is sometimes invoked to justify abortion or euthanasia, each of which might be said to clash with the commandment, 'You shall not murder.'

i) Autonomy and the respect for autonomy is respect for the individual, with treatment given if it is in the patient's best interest and where informed consent has been freely given. This links in with Paul's teaching from Philippians 2.4: 'Each of you should look not only to your own interests, but also to the interests of others' and with loving our neighbours as ourselves and the respect that should engender. Failing to give true informed consent can be equated to bearing false witness.

ii) and iii) Non-maleficence and beneficence are two sides of the same coin. Non-maleficence or *primum non nocere* is first of all to do no harm, whilst beneficence is to do good. Any surgical procedure or drug treatment has the potential to cause harm as well as do good. It is important to look at the risks and benefits and ensure that the benefits outweigh the risks. These principles can again be linked biblically. The sixth commandment, 'You shall not murder' is the ultimate command to do no harm whilst the desire to do good is enshrined in the healing ministry of Jesus. In a different context the writer to the Hebrews writes about God disciplining his children for good and that 'No discipline seems pleasant at the time, but painful' (Hebrews 12.11a). This perhaps helps to explain the dichotomy that a treatment can cause harm as well as do good.

iv) Justice means that any treatment should be given irrespective of age, gender or race. This is supported in Scripture by the principle that all human beings are equal in God's sight and should therefore have equal rights and responsibilities without prejudice.

The three key ethical areas to which the above principles should be applied are death, respect for persons and allocation of resources.

Death

Death is an inevitable part of life; it can be hastened or sometimes delayed, but without exception it happens to everyone. It can be expected or unexpected and is no respecter of age, gender, religion, race or social standing.

How Can Death Be Defined?

The common view is that death occurs when the heart stops beating and breathing ceases. But this is a simplified view and a better definition is that death is the irreversible loss of the capacity for consciousness combined with the irreversible loss of the capacity to breathe spontaneously and hence to maintain a spontaneous heart beat.[1] These criteria can usually be applied without difficulty. But there is a small group of patients who sustain an irreversible brain injury and as a result of prompt medical intervention are put onto a ventilator which takes over the breathing before the heart stops. As a result the concept of brain stem death has been developed.

The brain stem is the part of the brain that controls the vital functions such as the drive to breathe, maintaining blood pressure and the capacity for consciousness. Once the brain stem is dead the heart will stop beating shortly afterwards. There are a number of preconditions, necessary exclusions and tests to be performed which allow the diagnosis of brain stem death to be made. Provided

1 C Pallis and D H Harley, *ABC of Brainstem Death* (London: BMJ Publishing Group, 1996) pp 1–7.

these stringent conditions are met there is no prospect of recovery.[2] It is for this reason that the criteria of brain stem death are generally accepted for the diagnosis of death by the church and the legal and medical professions in the UK as well as in Europe and North America. It is important to ensure that the process of dying and death is independent of organ donation.

It should be acknowledged that there is a minority dissenting view. Some philosophers, such as Jonas and Singer, and a handful of doctors, have concerns about the validity of these criteria and would argue that these are prognostic (assessing what *will* happen) rather than diagnostic (assessing what *has* happened) criteria. They view cessation of all brain function as a transient stage in the process of dying, but not as the point of death, even though death is inevitable. Furthermore they argue that the life support machine (ventilator) be switched off and the patient be allowed to die peacefully.[3]

What Happens to the Body After Death?

There are many individual, cultural and religious views about what happens to the human body after death. This is closely linked with the concept of bodily integrity and the faith or otherwise that an individual and their family have.

i) Bodily integrity is to do with the body and its constituent parts being undisturbed and undamaged. Bodily integrity can be transgressed in life by therapeutic surgical procedures *eg* amputation of a limb and mastectomy and also after death by post-mortem and organ removal for transplantation. The concept of bodily integrity should not be dismissed lightly as each major religion has specific views about bodily integrity because of different beliefs about the body's ongoing role after death.

ii) For the Christian, death is not the end and there is the sure hope and promise of eternal life. Is the physical body needed after death? If so, how can it survive without organs that have been removed in life or after death? Paul writes in the letter to the Corinthians, 'Now we know that if the earthly tent we live in is destroyed, we have a building from God, an eternal house in heaven, not built by human hands' (1 Corinthians 5.1–5). 'There will be a resurrection of the human body—we will all be changed' (1 Corinthians 15.51). It is clear then from Scripture, that the physical body is changed after physical death and that there is no evidence that the spiritual body is located in any particular part of the physical body. Despite this there is an inherent value to the body and that it should be treated with respect. Humankind is made in the image of God and in the words of the psalmist is '...fearfully and wonderfully made' (Psalm 139.14). The body therefore demands respect and dignity in life, in dying and in death.

2   C Pallis and D H Harley, *ABC of Brainstem Death* (London: BMJ Publishing Group, 1996) pp 30–32.
3   P Singer, *Rethinking Life & Death* (Oxford: OUP, 1994) pp 20–37. M Evans, 'Against Brainstem Death' in R Gillon (ed), *Principles of Health Care Ethics* (Chichester: John Wiley and Sons, 1994).

Respect for Persons

The rights of an individual have come increasingly to the forefront with the introduction of the Equal Opportunities Act and latterly the Human Rights Act. Closely linked to the rights of an individual is the respect for and responsibilities of the individual. All individuals should be afforded the same degree of respect within society irrespective of gender, race, age and religion. Respect for others should be a basic tenet of any society. It is enshrined within Old and New Testament teachings and is summarized in the words of Jesus, 'So in everything, do to others what you would have them do to you, for this sums up the Law and the Prophets' (Matthew 7.12).

Rights and Responsibilities

Within transplantation the rights and responsibilities of individual parties may be in tension. The significant individual parties include the organ donor and their family and the transplant recipient and their family. The potential organ donor has the right to donate or not; their relatives have the right to give consent or not; the recipient of the transplant has the wish to have a transplant and the right to refuse one; the relatives of the recipient will want to have the best treatment for their loved one. These rights and associated responsibilities will differ with cadaveric and live donor transplants. Although each individual has rights, they also have responsibilities to themselves and to others. These responsibilities include respecting the wishes of others and helping others. Involved health care professionals also have responsibilities, which are primarily directed towards their patients.

To Whom Does the Body Belong?

When a cadaveric donor is considered, the body cannot 'belong' to the individual who is now dead. Although the ownership of the physical body is defined in legal terms, the decision to donate will usually be made by the next of kin. It is clear that the wishes of a potential donor to donate (and the agreement of their relatives) stems from a desire and a responsibility to help others. In this situation the rights and responsibilities of the potential donor have priority over those of the recipient. When a living donor is being considered the body belongs to the individual wishing to donate the organ who feels a responsibility to help their family.

The Christian would argue that the body belongs to God rather than to the individual. Paul encompasses this concept when he writes, 'Do you not know that your body is a temple of the Holy Spirit, who is in you, whom you have received from God? You are not your own; you were bought at a price. Therefore honour God with your body' (1 Corinthians 6.19). In this situation individuals have a responsibility to use their body in a way that is pleasing to God, which will often mean using it to the service of fellow human beings.

To Donate or Not to Donate

Individuals have an inherent free will and are free to choose whether they donate an organ or tissue. The decision to donate can include: donating a pint of blood; signing on to the organ donor register stating they would like to donate their organs when they die; donating part of a lung to a child in need; or equally deciding not to donate anything at all in life or in death. Choices can be made that are not fully informed and that have a significant impact upon both the individual and others. If this is the case then the rights of an individual can appear selfish. There is also the underlying responsibility to help others and respect the wishes of others. Paul writes, 'Each of you should look not only to your own interests, but also to the interests of others' (Philippians 2.4). There is a further perspective for the Christian to consider if the body belongs to God. The choices about donation are concerned with discerning the will of God in a particular situation. Individual Christians should prayerfully consider their own responsibilities and responses to the choices that relate to potential donation.

Informed Consent

In choices relating to donating or receiving an organ, it is important that the individual and his or her family are fully aware of all the implications of their decision. This is particularly important in live donor transplantation where the potential donor is having an operation (with its attendant risks) that they themselves do not need. The issue of informed consent is currently extremely topical and this has coincided with a change in the doctor-patient relationship from paternalism to partnership. The media has highlighted serious breaches in the doctor-patient relationship, there is a more litigious atmosphere and with the Internet there is more information available. As a result true informed consent is now more the norm and is a welcome development. There are limitations to informed consent, which relate to how effectively the appropriate information is given and received. Informed consent should be given in a way that is understandable to the person and allows adequate time for an informed decision to be made. This includes the requirements when minors or those who are mentally not able to give consent are involved. Messer gives a fuller account of consent in *The Therapeutic Covenant*.[4]

Allocation of Resources

This is a large topic, the detail of which is outside the scope of this booklet. However, the salient features should be considered as part of the ethical framework needed for transplantation. The two scarcest resources within transplantation are funding and organs.

---

4   N G Messer, *The Therapeutic Covenant* (Grove Ethical Studies booklet E 103).

Funding of Healthcare

Funding is a very complex issue, with no healthcare system in the world having sufficient funding to do all that can be done. Resource allocation is not just to do with the money but also how the money is used. The allocation of funding depends upon the healthcare system and in many areas of the world it is simply not appropriate to use limited resources on transplantation, which is expensive. This situation is therefore inherently unfair and unjust, but the unequal distribution of all resources across the global community is a much broader issue to which there are no simple answers. One approach is to apply the Parable of the Talents where more is expected of those who have most. We in the West have more money to spend on healthcare. We still have a responsibility to be good stewards of that, so that it is used in the most effective way, with a good return for patients, and not squandered.

Supply of Organs

Organs for transplantation are in short supply and throughout the world fewer cadaveric organs are becoming available for transplantation. As a consequence of this more live donor transplants are being performed. For kidney transplantation, live donors account for 40% of all transplants in Norway, 25–30% in USA and currently 20% in the UK and rising. Since there is an inadequate number of organs to meet the demand it is important that they should be allocated in a fair and equitable way to those individuals in whom the organ has the best chance of working long term, or where it is truly life saving and where the benefits outweigh the risks.

What is the Ethical Framework?

In concluding this chapter we have seen that the overarching biblical ethical principles are love for God and others. This is manifested as obedience to God and his commandments, service and self-sacrifice, justice and unconditional respect for others. These principles are intertwined with the four secular medical ethical principles of autonomy, non-maleficence, beneficence and justice.

Death is an inevitable part of life. There is a generally agreed and accepted definition of death including brain stem death, for which stringent conditions must be met. It is important to ensure that the process of dying and death is independent of organ donation in that full appropriate treatment is given until death occurs. If death is hastened to permit organ donation then this is in violation of the sixth commandment and the principle of autonomy and non-maleficence. From Scripture it seems that our resurrection bodies will be different from our physical pre-mortem bodies. The Christian basis for this is found in Paul's writings in 1 Corinthians 15.35–38 and 2 Corinthians 5.1–10. There would appear to be no scriptural contra-indication to cadaveric organ donation provided that the above principles are adhered to.

There is a great need to have a respect for persons regardless of status. Individuals have rights and responsibilities, but these are often complex, interrelated and in tension with each other. These rights and responsibilities need to be informed and exercised in a way that shows respect for others. Furthermore the body is a temple of the Holy Spirit and as such belongs to God. Any decision regarding organ donation should also be glorifying to God. There is a strong gifting principle associated with organ donation and the rights and responsibilities of the potential donor should always supersede those of the recipient. Organ donation and transplantation should only be undertaken where true informed consent has been obtained and an informed choice made, where the potential benefits outweigh the risks, the process is legal, and where there is not a significant negative impact upon other individuals. The key biblical themes are 'Do as you would have others to do unto you' (Matthew 7.12) and, 'Each of you should look not only to your own interests, but also to the interests of others.' (Philippians 2.4). These link in with the principles of autonomy, non-maleficence and beneficence.

The allocation of resources is a complex area; resources are finite and not everything is possible. As a result, the expectations of healthcare professionals, patients and their carers cannot always be met. The ethical principle of justice needs to be applied in this scenario. Choices have to be made about how funding and organs are allocated. This must be done in a way that is objective, fair, evidence-based, and where a good outcome is likely. The Parable of the Talents tells us to be good stewards of what we are given.

In this chapter I have endeavoured to apply biblical and secular medical ethical principles to each of the key issues. The resultant ethical framework, as summarized above, is now used to look at specific issues from the donor and recipient perspective and other new developments.

2
The Donor Perspective

The number of cadaveric organs for transplantation is decreasing and as a result three areas have been considered to expand the pool of available organs: the different types of cadaveric donor; changes to the law relating to organ donation; and live donors. These areas raise different ethical, moral and legal responses, but it is clear that the end should not justify the means. Transplantation should not be undertaken, no matter how necessary it is perceived, without the donor organ having been removed lawfully and ethically.

Cadaveric Organ Donors
Setting the Scene

Cadaveric organ donors can be heart beating or non-heart beating. The former are the commonest source of cadaveric organs for transplantation, but only a small proportion of patients dying in hospital with brain stem death are suitable. The patient is legally dead at this stage even though the heart continues beating whilst the ventilator maintains breathing. If the next of kin give consent for organ donation, the patient is then transferred to the operating theatre where the organs are removed and the ventilator stopped. If consent is not given the ventilator is turned off. This is existing practice throughout the UK, Europe and North America. There are two ethical issues that relate to this.

a) Is the patient dead when a diagnosis of brain stem death is made?

As we saw above (chapter 2), the consensus view is that a diagnosis of brain stem death is incompatible with life. The real issue is whether death should be regarded as an event or as a process. If death is a process then at what stage does it actually occur? Singer raises three questions that should be answered:

- When does a human being die?
- When is it permissible to stop trying to keep a human being alive?
- When is it permissible to remove organs from a human being for the purpose of transplantation to another human being?[5]

These are not simple questions, but nevertheless do need to be thought through, even if a definite answer cannot be given. According to the majority view, the answer to all three questions is when a diagnosis of brain stem death has been made.

---

5   P Singer, *Rethinking Life and Death* (Oxford: OUP, 1994) pp 54–56.

b) If the patient had expressed a wish to donate or not whilst alive, should that wish be honoured after death?

In the UK an 'opt-in' system is operated, so that if the individual has expressed a wish to donate *and* the family are asked by the hospital staff *and* the family give consent, then organ donation can go ahead. The individual can decide in life whether they would like to donate their organs in the event of their death and help someone else to enjoy the gift of life. But that positive decision can still be vetoed after death either knowingly by the family who have to give consent or unknowingly by medical staff who do not ask or consider the possibility of organ donation. The next of kin do have a legal right to refuse consent and in that time of grief it would be wrong to try too hard to persuade them. It can work the other way round when the individual has expressed a wish not to donate, but the family reverses that wish when asked. The key principle here is of respect for the wishes of others and that respect should count for more than rights.

Different Types of Cadaveric Donor

The number of organs from conventional cadaveric heart-beating donors has steadily declined in the UK from a peak in 1990. The reasons for this have already been alluded to, but the resultant effect is that fewer cadaveric organ transplants are performed whilst more people are waiting or dying whilst waiting. As a result other types of cadaveric donors have been considered, but because of medical reasons are only really appropriate for patients awaiting a kidney transplant. These include organs from marginal donors, non-heart-beating donors and where interventional ventilation has occurred.

a) Marginal Donors

These are conventional heart-beating donors or controlled non-heart-beating donors (see below), but whose organs are sub-optimal because of the age or medical condition of the donor. Formerly these organs would not have been used, but because of the shortage may now be used in selected recipients. The ethical debate about using these donors really relates to the recipient who is going to receive them and consequently will be dealt with in more detail in chapter 4.

b) Non-heart-beating Donors

In the controlled situation, a patient with irreversible brain damage who does not meet the criteria for brain stem death has their life support withdrawn after discussion with the family. The heart stops, death is diagnosed and the kidneys can be removed with consent. In the uncontrolled situation, a patient arrives in an Accident and Emergency Department and is dead on arrival or dies shortly afterwards. When death has been confirmed a small tube is placed into a main artery in the groin and cold fluid run through to cool and preserve the kidneys. Consent is then sought from the next of kin. If this is granted then the patient is taken to theatre and the kidneys removed; if it is refused then the tube is removed. The two main ethical issues are:

i) *Is it ethical to insert the tube to cool the kidneys without consent when it is not for the benefit of the patient?*

From a practical point of view unless the tube is inserted at the beginning and the kidneys quickly cooled then the organs will be unusable. If the individual had expressed a desire to donate in life and the family are in agreement, then unless the tube is inserted, this wish cannot be fulfilled. On the other hand it would not seem ethical for the tube to be inserted without permission from the next of kin when it was unnecessary for the patient's treatment. Are the needs of the potential transplant recipient greater than the rights of the potential donor and the family?

ii) *Can distressed relatives give true informed consent when a rapid decision is required?*

The dilemma can also be applied to other situations where patients are critically ill and require urgent medical intervention. Superficially it is difficult to see how distressed relatives can give true informed consent as their judgment may be clouded, they may not hear all the facts or have adequate time to think through all the implications. Yet in this situation the option is either not to go ahead with organ donation and subsequent transplantation or to give the options clearly and simply and offer ongoing support in that decision. If families have already discussed organ donation the decision is made easier. Furthermore, allowing the organs to be given to someone in need can be a highly positive and rewarding action that can help in the bereavement process. Families should be given the opportunity to decide about organ donation provided it is done in a sensitive, respectful manner with no pressure to say yes or no.

c) Interventional Ventilation

Interventional ventilation was practised in Exeter a decade ago where it had a significant impact upon the local organ retrieval rates. The background to this was that a number of patients died on medical wards with severe strokes or brain haemorrhages. When the patient was in the terminal phase of this and where the relatives were in agreement, the patient would be moved to the intensive care unit and put on a life support machine. The patient would then be ventilated until such a time that the criteria for brain stem death were met and the organs then removed. The potential to expand its use to other centres in the UK initiated a huge debate around ethical, legal, logistic and resource issues to such an extent that it was essentially deemed illegal. Ethical issues raised included:

* This issue of consent and treatment not for the patient's own benefit;
* The use of a scarce intensive care bed, which may deprive a recoverable patient of it;
* The risk of the patient developing a persistent vegetative state and not becoming brain dead.

Changes to the Law Relating to Organ Donation

The laws relating to organ donation vary from country to country. In the UK an opting-in system is in place. The advantages of the system are that it allows individuals and their families to make a positive choice about organ donation one way or another. There is usually adequate time to obtain proper informed consent and if consent is given there is the sense that someone else has been helped and often given the 'gift of life.' However, because of the shortfall in cadaveric organs for transplantation, changes to the law have been proposed and have been introduced in other countries. The two major changes concern required request and presumed consent.

Required Request

This law, which has been introduced in parts of the USA, makes it mandatory for a doctor to ask for consent for organ donation from the next of kin of suitable patients. However, in other countries doctors are not required to ask and as a result some patients will not become organ donors who would be suitable. There may be various reasons why the family are not asked but it will usually be an act of omission rather than commission. The protagonists argue that introducing such a law would ensure that families of all suitable patients are asked to consider organ donation and that this may increase the number of organ donors. Some families have been upset that organ donation was not discussed with them and that the opportunity was lost. Furthermore, if the patient had previously expressed a wish to donate and if their next of kin are not asked then the patient's wish could not be fulfilled. The opposing view is that doctors do not like being told what to do and if required to ask might do so in such a way that consent would not be obtained. There may also be occasions where the doctor caring for a patient genuinely believes that it would be harmful for the family to be asked about organ donation. In reality, introducing a law of required request would be an attempt to enforce what should already be good practice. A more simple approach may be to better educate and train those health care professionals in the front line so that they are fully aware of organ donation and transplantation and how to break bad news and talk about donation in a respectful and sympathetic manner.

Presumed Consent

Presumed consent has been debated widely in the UK over the last couple of years. It has been the law in a number of European countries, most notably Austria and Belgium, for some years. In these countries the organ donation rate is higher, but there are other compounding factors such as a higher rate of fatal road accidents compared with the UK. Presumed consent, or 'opting out,' assumes that the individual is willing to give consent for organ donation, unless they have specifically opted out and registered that objection on a central registry. In those countries where this law is in operation only a small proportion of people register, as the majority will never get around to it. For that majority it cannot be assumed that they are giving informed consent, as they are unlikely to have thought actively about it. In practice this law is rarely enforced, because of reluctance within the medical and legal professions to do so and an unwillingness to veto the wishes of relatives. There is concern that by enforcing the law there could be a resultant adverse impact upon transplantation. The key ethical considerations are:

a) Is Presumed Consent the Same as Informed Consent?

Presumed consent is only informed consent if everyone under the jurisdiction of the law is fully aware of the implications of opting in or out. This relies upon effective publicity and information plus a reliable infrastructure to maintain and access the register. The population must be suitably motivated to access the information and make a conscious decision one way or another. Any other national law (such as having a television licence or keeping within the speed limit) requires clear compliance and if the law is not kept there are penalties. This is not the case with presumed consent as the penalty of failing to act upon the law may result in the individual's organs being used after death irrespective of their wishes. There would be no chance of a suspended sentence! On that basis it is difficult to see how it can be informed consent. However, in those countries where the law is in place there does not seem to been an adverse impact upon transplantation, but this is probably because the wishes of the relatives are not vetoed.

b) Is Presumed Consent the First Step to Routine Removal of Organs from All Suitable Patients?

The central ethical issue is whether the individual, the family, the state or God has moral claim on the body, when the body can be used for the benefit of others. In this situation it is important to show respect for the wishes of the person and the family and therefore it is not right for the state to demand donation. P Ramsey writes 'the routine taking of organs would deprive individuals of the exercise of the virtue of generosity.'[6] The routine removal of organs would appear unethical as it transgresses the rights and responsibilities of the donor and is unlikely to be supported by the majority of the public or healthcare professionals. This has been highlighted recently with the controversy around the retention of organs at Alder Hey and other hospitals. Presumed consent is a separate entity, as individuals would still have a choice.

Living Organ Donors

The first successful kidney transplant was performed between twins in Boston in 1954 and recently live donor transplants have also been performed using parts of the liver, lung and small bowel. With the increasing demand for transplantation and fewer cadaveric organs available the rate of live donor transplantation is increasing. There are significant advantages for both donor and recipient as the donor can do something positive to help and outcomes are better. However, there are disadvantages as the donor is having a major operation with the

---

6   P Ramsey, *The Patient as Person: Explorations in Medical Ethics* (New Haven: Yale, 1970) p 210.

attendant risks. The general ethical issues around living donors will be considered as well as specific issues relating to the type of donor.

The Ethics of Living Organ Donation

The central ethical issue is that people are submitting themselves to a major operation that they do not need. The major issue that needs to be considered is the small risk of death, which for removal of a kidney is in the order of 1 in 1600–3000. As liver lobes, lung lobes and small bowel may now be removed the risk of death will increase. What is an acceptable risk? The risks of any procedure need to be minimized. Extensive tests will be performed to ensure that the donor and their organs are fit and healthy. There must be no coercion, pressure or financial inducements. The gift of the organ must be freely given. This is why informed consent is crucial—the patient and the extended family need to be fully aware of all the risks involved. If the potential donor, recipient, their families or the healthcare team looking after them have any doubts, then the donation and transplant should not go ahead. The risks, provided they are not excessive, will usually be outweighed by the benefit to the recipient who can be restored to health with positive benefits for the whole family. In some situations it will be positively life saving. The love and responsibility to the family can be summed up in John 15.13, 'Greater love has no-one than this, that he lay down his life for his friend'—although the medical profession would not allow donation to proceed if there was a significant risk of death! It is more difficult when the potential donor is a child, for example the twin of the patient, or mentally incapable of giving consent. A number of precedents have been set where the wider family are in agreement but where independent guardians have been appointed and legal approval gained.

Types of Living Organ Donors

There is a wide variety of living donor transplants being performed throughout the world ranging from the ethically acceptable to the ethically unacceptable. These fall into three main categories.

a) Living Related Donors (LRD) and Living Unrelated but Emotionally Related Donors (LURD)

These are the conventional type of living donors and the relationships are defined in the Human Organ Transplant Act (1989). The usual relationships for the LRD are sibling-sibling or parent-child, but may also be child-parent, aunt/uncle–niece/nephew and first cousins. The LURD relationship includes spouse-spouse, brother/sister-in law, grandparent-child and close friends. The ethical issues raised have already been dealt with above and this process is generally viewed as being ethically acceptable. One area that requires closer examination is where close friends are being considered. The relationship needs to be looked at carefully and in particular the motivation behind the offer. One case that aroused considerable media interest was where a bishop with kidney failure was offered a kidney by one of his congregation. It could be argued that although the potential donor felt a responsibility to donate, the potential recipient could also have a responsibility to accept or decline the offer. There are also legal requirements to be fulfilled to ensure that the donor and recipient are in the relationship claimed. If the risks are minimized then there is the potential for the donor to do 'a very beautiful thing' for their loved one.

b) Altruistic Donor

The altruistic donor is one who wishes to donate an organ to anyone who may benefit. This type of donation has also been called Samaritan donation. Any blood donor is an altruistic donor, but where solid organs are concerned an individual can only be an altruistic donor once! There are different types of altruistic donor that can be considered.

i) Non-directed altruism—an offer to donate an organ, which goes to the best person in the general pool of recipients and is therefore not known to the recipient.
ii) Directed altruism—an offer to donate an organ to a specific individual or type of individual *eg* children or to another Christian. Within the last year there was the example of a man who donated a lobe of his lung to help a child in the USA who needed a lung transplant. It may be better to consider this type of donation as a *friend to friend* LURD
iii) Paired donation—a pair who cannot donate one to the other being matched with another similar pair and the donated kidneys exchanged.

The key issue with altruistic donation is to determine what motivates the individual. Some would argue that to undergo voluntarily a major operation with its attendant risks to benefit a stranger must mean that the donor is foolish or mad! Although this may sometimes be the case, there may simply be the desire to help another fellow being, a virtue that is found in those of all faiths and none. For each type there may be different motivational factors that need to be thoroughly explored. Providing that there is proper informed consent, the donor is of sound mind and offering from purely altruistic motives and that the organ goes unconditionally to the person who would gain most benefit, then there may be no major ethical objections. However, it is not legal in the UK and there would be considerable opposition from the medical profession.

c) Commercialism

There is an urban legend that tells of a young man who goes to a nightclub one night. The next thing he remembers is waking up the next morning by the side of the road with a pain in his side. When he looks there is a surgical incision there and when he attends the casualty department he discovers that a kidney has been removed. Although this is fiction, there appears to be a trade in organs in some Eastern European countries. There have been recent reports of organ trafficking in Moldova (BBC TV *Newsnight*, July 9, 2001) and people being killed and their organs removed in Uzbekistan (*Sunday Times*, July 29, 2001). In China, organs of executed prisoners are apparently sold for purposes of transplantation. The buying and selling of organs is prohibited by law in many countries of the world and strongly opposed by the various international transplant organizations, but is still practised openly in parts of Asia. The common scenario is for a rich person with kidney failure to buy a kidney from a poor person who wants to sell one of theirs, with the deal brokered by a middleman. The rich person will be a bit poorer but will have a transplant with a resulting improved quality of life; the poor person will be richer by the equivalent of a year's wages, which may help educate children or provide healthcare; whilst the middleman is considerably richer and has a lucrative business. From the utilitarian principle, if everybody is happy, then what is the problem?

There are of course some fundamental issues at stake:

i) Selling an organ takes away the gifting principle and cheapens the value of the human body, which is made in the image of God. There is also the concern about whether these donors get adequate medical care before and after surgery and are able to give full informed consent.

ii) The middleman is making a large profit so that the recipient pays over the odds, whilst the donor is inadequately compensated. This situation is repeated countless times within other parts of the global economy where the poor are exploited.

iii) Organs are a scarce resource and should be distributed fairly, irrespective of age, gender and race, not in accordance with one's ability to pay for them. This argument is easy to apply in the West, but if you live in a country with inadequate dialysis facilities, no cadaveric transplant programme and no suitable relative to donate an organ then the choices can be limited. It may simply be a choice between life and death, where the cost of life is the cost of a transplant. There are huge global differences in healthcare provision. There is a disparity between the wealthy buyer's choice and the potential donor's choice —the ability to exercise choice and the determining factors in making a decision are linked to their respective social situations.

One other aspect to be considered is the compensation of the donor for loss of earnings and travel expenses. However, if this compensation comes from the donor or recipient family or from the hospital concerned it could be viewed as an inducement. This could potentially remove the altruistic nature of the donation and raise concerns about whether there was coercion. There are equally others who would argue that this is a very reasonable approach. A more detailed account of the ethics involved in buying and selling organs is given by Brecher and Sells.[7]

---

7   See B Brecher, 'Organs for Transplant: donation or payment?' and R A Sells, 'Transplants' both in R Gillon (ed) *Principles of Health Care Ethics* (Chichester: John Wiley and Sons, 1994) pp 993–1002 and1003–1025.

3
The Recipient Perspective

It is not surprising that most of the ethical dilemmas relate to donors, as they have least to gain from transplantation. However, there are significant ethical issues from the recipient's perspective, which focus on selection (who goes on the list) and allocation criteria (who gets any individual organ).

Selection Criteria

Not everyone who develops end organ failure is suitable for transplantation. There are some absolute and relative contra-indications to transplantation. There are a number of underlying principles that should be applied in deciding which patients should go on the transplant list.

The Potential Benefits of the Transplant Should Outweigh the Risks

A patient should only be put on the transplant list if the potential benefit of being alive with a working transplant and an improved quality of life is greater than the risk of death or serious complications or a worse quality of life. The ethical principles of beneficence and non-maleficence operate here. A transplant is not necessarily the end to a patient's problem and should be viewed as a treatment rather than a cure. A patient may insist that they want the chance of a transplant whatever the risk and that that is their right. The doctor has a duty of care and if there is a significant risk of doing more harm than good, then the patient's wishes cannot be met. Within this partnership the patient needs to be shown respect, but neither should the doctor contravene the spirit of the sixth commandment. If a patient dies soon after a transplant, with that transplant still working then it can be considered a waste of that organ and of the other resources invested in it. With an increasing shortage of organs this perhaps has to be a more important consideration. Just because a transplant *can* be performed on an individual does not mean that it *should* be.

With Organs Scarce, a Reasonable Length of Survival Should be Anticipated

This aspect has just been briefly mentioned, but there are a number of important factors that can shorten the life of the transplant. These include both factors that the patient has control over (compliance with treatment and self-inflicted diseases) or no control over (previous transplants, mental incapacity and recurrent disease in the transplant). If organs are in short supply should the organ be given to the person in whom it is going to last the longest or to the person who is in most need irrespective of how long the organ will last? In the latter case the choice may literally be death or a couple of years of added life before the transplant fails or the patient dies. When faced with the individual these are not easy decisions to make, but there are perhaps some principles than can apply.

19

i) The patient may demonstrate poor compliance with treatment by poor hospital attendances and failing to take medication, or the primary organ damage is self-inflicted such as with alcoholic liver disease. In these situations, transplantation should probably not be considered unless the patient demonstrates some commitment and responsibility to change of lifestyle and attitude. Jesus cares for these modern day outcasts. Society and the Christian community have a responsibility to care and help in lifestyle modification.

ii) If the patient has had previous transplants or there is the likelihood of recurrent disease then the risks of success and failure need to be openly discussed by the patient and the clinician. If there is a reasonable chance of success and the patient has been fully informed of the risks then it is probably reasonable to consider transplantation.

iii) Where the patient is mentally incapable of making a decision, the decision should be made on the basis of the support that the patient's carer(s) can give in both the short and long term. In general, compliance with treatment is faultless in this group of patients. All individuals are equal in God's sight and transplantation should not be denied solely on the basis of mental state.

The Decision Should be a Joint One Between the Clinician and the Patient

One of the current themes in the new style NHS is partnership, although this is not a new concept.[8] Indeed partnership is a recurrent biblical theme. Any decision about whether a patient goes on the transplant list should be a joint decision between the clinician, patient and often the family. All parties need to be fully informed of the risks and benefits and need to respect the views of the other.

Allocation Criteria

The allocation criteria only apply to cadaveric organs and in the UK there are defined rules as to which patient gets any particular organ. These criteria are objective and are nationally agreed but differ from organ to organ. These have been most well developed in kidney transplantation where allocation is based primarily on those factors that equate with the best outcome. Although there would seem to be no ethical concerns with the above arrangement, there are two particular areas of ethical debate.

Equality of Access

In 1999 conditional organ donation made the media headlines when a family agreed for the organs of a loved one to be donated provided they went to a recipient of a similar race. In that situation the request was followed through and not surprisingly a wide debate ensued. An enquiry was set up which subsequently reported and reiterated that conditional organ donation should not happen. The general consensus amongst the transplant community was that if relatives put conditions on donation then that donation should not occur. It is encouraging to

---

8   P Ramsey, *The Patient as Person: Explorations in Medical Ethics* (New Haven: Yale, 1970) p 6.

see that in that scenario ethical principles were more important than organ dona-tion, even in the face of shortage. Equality of access to organs is a fundamental ethical principle that should be applied, but that for reasons already explained cannot be applied across the whole global community. All are equal in the sight of God irrespective of age, gender, race or area of residence and this principle should be applied wherever possible. It must be recognized, however, that there will always be groups who are inherently disadvantaged because of difficulty in finding 'matches' and others who will not even meet the criteria to be suitable for a transplant.

Allocation of Organs from 'Marginal Donors'

With the shortage of cadaveric organs, donors are being used where there is the potential for the organs to be sub-optimal. Non-heart beating donors have already been discussed, but organs from the elderly and others where quality is not so good are also being used. This raises the question as to whether the poten-tial recipient should be informed and therefore make a choice as to whether ac-cept that kidney or not. If information is knowingly withheld this can be equated with bearing false witness and not showing love and respect.

4
What Next?

The preceding chapters have looked at ethical issues that relate to existing practice within transplantation. With the increasing scarceness of organs for transplantation, rising waiting lists and increased public expectation, other ways of providing organs for transplantation are being developed. These have already and will continue to raise even greater ethical dilemmas. Ridley has stated that, 'some of the issues specific to procuring and transplanting bodily organs only arise because organs are a scarce resource.'[9] A brief resume of these clinical areas and the ethical issues raised are outlined below. It is likely that the ethical framework developed in this book will be insufficient to deal with some of these issues and will need to be expanded.

Anencephalic Donors[10]
Anencephalic babies are born with a brain stem, but without a higher brain. These babies will inevitably die soon after birth. Normally termination of pregnancy will be offered to these mothers, but if declined the baby will be born and could be considered for organ donation. Since the brain stem is present, brain stem death cannot be diagnosed. This causes ethical and legal difficulties in deciding whether these babies are suitable for organ donation.

Foetal Brain Transplants[11]
Tissue from aborted foetuses has been used for research and therapeutic purposes. Foetal brain tissue has been used in the treatment of Parkinson's disease by transplanting the cells. It has also been suggested that with further advances it may be possible to grow organs from foetal cells, with the possibility that they can be used for transplantation. A man may have kidney failure and be waiting for a transplant. His wife may therefore conceive, have an abortion so that the foetal cells can be grown into kidney, which can then be transplanted into her husband.[12] It may sound far-fetched, but the technology is not far off. There are huge ethical ramifications for this.

Xenotransplantation
This is the transplantation of organs from one species to another. There have been a number of cases of baboon-to-human liver and heart transplants in the United States, but none of them have been successful in the medium to long

---

9   A Ridley, *Beginning Bioethics—A Text with Integrated Readings* (New York: St. Martin's Press, 1998) p 256.
10 A Sommerville, *Medical Ethics Today: Its practice and philosophy* (London: BMJ Publishing Group,1993) p 27.
11 Sommerville, *Medical Ethics Today*, p 29.
12 Ridley, *Beginning Bioethics*, pp 262–264.

term. Most of the experimental work is being done on pig-to-human transplants and the three main challenges are overcoming rejection, the risk of transmitting pig infections into the human population and the ethical implications. There is a whole range of ethical questions to be asked. Should animal organs be used for human transplants? Should animals be specifically bred and genetically engineered for transplantation? Will it be safe for the individual and the wider public? Will it be efficacious compared with human transplantation? Will it be acceptable to patients and their carers?

Genetic Engineering and Cloning

There have been major advances in this field, which have been touched upon above. There is significant concern that both genetic engineering and cloning can be construed as *playing God*. Pope John Paul II has said that attempts at human cloning with a view to obtain organs for transplantation, insofar as they involve the manipulation and destruction of human embryos are not morally acceptable, even when their proposed goal is good in itself.[13]

Resource Allocation

There are finite financial resources within the NHS, but what seems to be an infinite call upon them. Transplantation is a high-cost, 'high-tech' field and if genetic engineering, xenotransplantation and cloning are developed then will there be the resources for them to be implemented? Already an increasing number of powerful and effective anti-rejection drugs are becoming available, but the resources are not always available for them to be used. If they are used then it may be at the expense of another treatment for another group of patients. At the same time even basic healthcare cannot be provided in many countries of the world. Resource allocation is an increasing problem and there are some interesting ethical questions raised.

---

13   Pope John Paul II, *Address to the XVIII International Congress of the Transplantation Society, Rome 2000.* On the subject of human cloning, see further Neil Messer *The Ethics of Human Cloning* (Grove Ethics booklet E 122).

5
Conclusion

Transplantation is now an established form of treatment for patients with organ failure. In this booklet I have highlighted the major ethical issues that are encountered in current practice with particular respect to the donor and recipient. An ethical framework has been developed from the key issues of death, respect for persons and resource allocation. The key points of this framework are:

- The overarching biblical ethical principles are love for God and others and are manifested as obedience to God and his commandments, service and self-sacrifice, justice and unconditional respect for others.
- It needs to be recognized that individuals have rights and responsibilities, but the body ultimately belongs to God and that fully informed choices should be made in that light.
- There is a strong gifting principle associated with organ donation and the rights and responsibilities of the potential donor should always supersede those of the recipient.
- Choices have to be made about how funding and organs are allocated and this should be done in a way that is objective, fair, based on evidence and where a good outcome is likely.

I have endeavoured to apply that framework in a balanced manner recognizing those areas where there are no simple answers, and where some principles have been laid down.

The demand for transplantation outweighs the supply of resources, especially organs. As a result new options are being proposed for cadaveric and live donors and the legal framework. The developed ethical framework has also been applied to those areas. With new and emergent technology, for example xenotransplantation, genetic engineering and cloning, new ethical issues are raised. It is likely that the developed ethical framework will need to be expanded to deal with these.

It is vitally important that ethical thinking keeps up to date with each new development. If not, these advances will take place within a moral vacuum. It is my hope that this booklet will encourage Christian thinking, involvement and influence in these areas.